Farewell
GIANTS STADIUM

THE CONCERTS, THE EVENTS, THE SPORTS

ACKNOWLEDGMENTS

This collection of photos, representing the more than 1,600 events held at Giants Stadium, captures some of the key events that have generated millions of memories, countless hours of enjoyment and smiles at Giants Stadium for everyone who entered its storied portals.

As Walt Disney once said, "You can dream, create, design and build the most wonderful place in the world, but it requires people to make the dream a reality."

This book is dedicated to the teams that have called Giants Stadium home and to the millions of fans, players, artists and employees who have made Giants Stadium that reality.

Thank you and enjoy these memories,

— Your friends at The Star-Ledger &
the Staff at Giants Stadium and The Meadowlands Sports Complex

Copyright© 2010 • ISBN: 978-1-59725-248-5

Published by Pediment Publishing, a division of The Pediment Group, Inc. www.pediment.com Printed in Canada

TABLE OF CONTENTS

FOREWORD

By Jerry Izenberg
The Star-Ledger's
Columnist Emeritus

There was a time when Wellington Mara, who owned the Giants, and Sonny Werblin, who then owned the Jets, were the most bitter of enemies, locked in an emotional, financial and artistic vendetta that begged the 100-yard pro football question: "Who owns New York?"

And all the while, clouded by the image of a fading Yankee Stadium, the real question went unnoticed, unconsidered and unanswered.

It should have been:

"Who wants it?"

Who wants the wall-to-wall parking lot that was the Major Deegan Expressway before and after game time? Who wants the bridge-and-tunnel tolls travelers from New Jersey and Connecticut, who made up roughly 45 percent of the auto traffic, had to pay? Who wants to pay a king's ransom to park the car in the first place? And so on and so on ...

Or, later, to paraphrase what Werblin, by then repatriated as former Jets owner but still a New Jersey citizen, said to then Gov. William T. Cahill ...

"If we build it, they'll all want to come."

It was then that the New Jersey Sports and Exposition Authority was born — and with it, the dream that made the Jersey Swamplands bloom.

On a gray November morning in 1972, Werblin and Mara, the two men who had once fought so bitterly during the war between the old-guard National Football League and the upstart American Football League, stepped into a slice of desolate swamp ... a slice of Jerseyana that offered all the majesty of a dirty dish rag in a pool of old coffee grounds.

Until this moment, the only digging ever done here was carried out by guys wearing expensive imported shoes conducting ad lib scientific experiments to see how far a rival mobster could sink into the swamp with a Wurlitzer jukebox chained to his ankles.

The minute Werblin, Mara and the Governor sank their shovels into what had formerly been a New Jersey no-man's land, everything changed. From all of this would rise Giants Stadium. It would tower over the horizon for more than three decades as powerful an emotional beacon as it was a physical one.

Through its completion and what it became, it sent a message both around the state and across the Hudson to Manhattan, and seemed to trumpet:

"We have seen our future, and you ain't in it. Say farewell to the Jets. They are coming here. Say farewell to the Cosmos. This is where they will play. Forget about the World Cup. It sets up shop here. You want to see Lawrence Taylor, Phil Simms, or a Super Bowl winner? This is the place. ... Madison Square Garden won't ever get the Final Four. Once we build a companion arena down the road, we will. Don't even think of ever calling us second class again."

And all across New Jersey the message was: "Finally ... finally ... something of our own. The Pope will say Mass here and 82,948 communicants will pray with him. The Boss will sing here — 24 times. Our high school kids will decide football championships here. Michael J. Fox and Muhammad Ali, partners in the battle against Parkinson's Disease, will speak here. So will the Rev. Billy Graham.

"It will host more NFL combined regular- and post-season games than any other stadium in the league's history. Pele will play his final game here and 76,000 fans will repeat after him with a roar that shook the building 'love ... love ... love.'"

From the moment the Giants played their first game here in 1976, the joint became New Jersey's staging ground for the spectacular. The Jackson 5 performed three shows of their Victory Tour here. Navy-Notre Dame and Army-Navy shook down the echoes with two of America's greatest football rivalries. Everybody who was anybody wanted a piece of center stage:

The Who, Bon Jovi, The Police, U2, Pink Floyd, Miles Davis, Grateful Dead, Madonna, The Rolling Stones, Kiss, Guns N' Roses, Paul McCartney, Billy Joel — and the rest of this list could fill a book of its own.

What other stadium could generate the distinct feeling that it was haunted? The furiously erratic winds inexplicably changed directions to foil the best-laid plans of field goal kickers almost as though the Great Oz was behind some curtain under the stands with a wind machine.

There were more than a few who swore the Giants deliberately opened a stadium door to compound this.

And there were others with an eerier explanation. This, urban legend-makers swore, was the final resting place of Jimmy Hoffa, the Teamsters chief whose body has never been found. Students of such folk myths insist it accounts for the number of fumbles on the 40-yard line or even that Giants' nightmare on the day Joe Pisarcik, the Giants' quarterback, snatched defeat from the jaws of victory on the final play of the game with an incredible botched handoff.

This place will be soon gone. A new supercalifragilistic stadium will rise in its place next door to be shared, as this one was, by the Giants and Jets.

But while it lasted, Giants Stadium was ours even when ill-fated football teams like the New Jersey Generals and the XFL's Hitmen briefly borrowed it.

If, as philosophers say, the past is prologue, let it never be forgotten that this place was our 100-yard Camelot.

October 1, 1977

Pelé's Farewell Game ::
A crowd of 75,646 fans filled Giants Stadium to bid farewell to soccer legend Pelé, who played one-half of his final game for the Cosmos and the second half for his former team, Santos of Brazil. (World Wide Television Broadcast)

October 10, 1976

Giants Stadium Opening Day ::
76,042 fans witnessed the Giants playing the Cowboys in the first game ever played at Giants Stadium.

August 14, 1977

Cosmos Win the NASL Atlantic Conference Championship :: The Cosmos prevailed over the Eastern Division Champion Ft. Lauderdale Strikers to an audience of 77,691 even though stadium capacity was only 76,891. This marked the first and only time that (800) tickets were sold as standing room only. The Cosmos would go on to win the Soccer Bowl of 1977.

August 27, 1978

Cosmos Win the NASL Soccer Bowl of 1978 :: NASL defending champions, the Cosmos, won the North American Soccer League's Soccer Bowl, defeating the Tampa Bay Rowdies 3-1 in front of a crowd of 74,901.

December 16, 1978

The first… Garden State Bowl :: The first of four Garden State Bowl games featured Rutgers losing to Arizona State, 34-18.

September 2, 1978

The first… Grateful Dead Concert :: Featuring Jerry Garcia and Bob Weir.

June 25, 1978

First Concert Ever Held at Giants Stadium :: The Beach Boys attracted 62,583 fans to the first concert in Giants Stadium history.

November 1, 1980

Navy vs. Notre Dame Game :: This was the first of six match-ups at Giants Stadium between the two iconic teams. Notre Dame 33, Navy 0.

March 20, 1983

The first… USFL New Jersey Generals Game :: The United States Football League's New Jersey Generals had their first ever home game at Giants Stadium against the Tampa Bay Bandits with Heisman Trophy winner Herschel Walker starting at running back.

August 7, 1982

FIFA World All-Star Game :: Played for the benefit of UNICEF, the game featured Europe vs. World All-Stars. Players included Diego Maradona, Zico, Giorgio Chinaglia, Paolo Rossi and Franz Beckenbauer. (World Wide Television Broadcast)

June 15, 1980

Music at the Meadowlands :: Featured The Eagles, Heart, Little River Band and 67,234 in attendance.

August 29, 1983

Kickoff Classic I :: The first of twenty Kickoff Classics featured the defending NCAA national champions, the Penn State Nittany Lions and the pre-season #1 ranked Nebraska Cornhuskers. The Cornhuskers were victorious, beating the Nittany Lions 44-6. Additionally, Kickoff Classic I was the first college football game to ever be played in August.

September 6, 1984

New York Jets move to New Jersey :: The Jets faced the Pittsburgh Steelers in their home opener at Giants Stadium.

July 14, 1985

The USFL Championship Game :: Baltimore Stars 28, Oakland Invaders 24

July 29-31, 1984

The Jackson 5 Victory Tour :: Giants Stadium was The Jacksons' fourth stop on their Victory Tour.

1970   1980

August - September, 1985

Bruce Springsteen & The E Street Band :: Born in the U.S.A. Tour – 6 Shows

January 27, 1987

New York Giants Super Bowl Victory Celebration :: The New York Giants, including Super Bowl MVP Phil Simms, celebrated their victory in Super Bowl XXI

June 29 - July 3, 1989

The Who in Concert :: The Who played 4 shows in 5 days on June 29-30 and July 2-3. Total Attendance: 223,135

October 15, 1985

New York Jets Retire Joe Namath's Number 12

January 4, 1987

New York Giants Divisional Playoff Game :: The New York Giants, who finished the regular season first in the NFC East with a record of 14-2, dominated the San Francisco 49er's 49-3.

August 30, 1987

Kickoff Classic V: Tennessee vs. Iowa :: With three seconds left in the game, Phil Reich kicked a game-winning field goal to lead the Tennessee Volunteers to a comeback victory 23-22 over the Iowa Hawkeyes.

June 11, 1989

Bon Jovi in Concert :: Set a concert attendance record: 72,641

June 15, 1986

A Conspiracy of Hope Tour :: The final of 6 concerts on the tour was played at Giants Stadium in an all-day event, to a sold-out audience. The concert, which was held on behalf of Amnesty International, broadcasted on MTV and was the only outdoor show of the tour. The final show featured many additional artists being that it lasted for 11 hours, but was headlined by U2, Sting, Bryan Adams, Joan Baez, Lou Reed, Peter Gabriel, The Neville Brothers, and a reunion of The Police.

September 14, 1987

U2 Concert :: The Joshua Tree Tour

December 29, 1985

The first... New York Giants Home Playoff Game :: Completing the regular season as NFC East Champions with a 10-6 record, the New York Giants won their first home playoff game at Giants Stadium 17-3 against the San Francisco 49ers who were led by Hall of Fame Quarterback Joe Montana.

January 11, 1987

New York Giants Conference Championship Game :: In what the late Wellington Mara called his fondest memory in their time in Giants Stadium, the New York Giants shutout their division rival, the Washington Redskins, 17-0 in the NFC Championship game. This resulted in the first Giants Super Bowl appearance in team history, followed by the first Giants Super Bowl victory.

December 9, 1989

The first... Army vs. Navy in Giants Stadium :: Navy won 19-17 due to Frank Schenk's 32 yard field goal with 11 seconds remaining.

December 28, 1985

The first... New York Jets Home Playoff Game :: After finishing the regular season with an 11-5 record, the New York Jets battled the New England Patriots in their first home playoff game at Giants Stadium.

July 6, 1986

Liberty Weekend Closing Ceremonies :: Liberty Weekend, the celebration of the Statue of Liberty Centennial and restoration of the statue, ended at Giants Stadium with a tribute to popular culture.

June 26, 1988

Monsters of Rock Tour :: The concert featured Van Halen (headline act), Metallica and Dokken.

August 28, 1991

Kickoff Classic IX :: With a share of the 1990 NCAA Football National Title, the Georgia Tech Yellow Jackets' 16 game unbeaten streak came to an end in their 1991 season opener, losing to the preseason #1 ranked Penn State Nittany Lions 34-22.

Summer of 1990

A Record-setting 10 Concerts in One Stadium :: No outdoor stadium had ever held 10 concerts in one summer. Fans were treated to two shows each from Billy Joel, Paul McCartney and New Kids on the Block and concerts by David Bowie, Depeche Mode, Amitabh Bachchan and Budweiser Superfest. Total Attendance: 480,907.

January 13, 1991

New York Giants vs. Chicago Bears – Divisional Playoff :: The New York Giants defeated the Chicago Bears 31-3 en route to winning Super Bowl XXV.

April 6, 1991

The first... New York/New Jersey Knights Game :: World League of American Football

August 4, 1994

Grateful Dead Concert :: The one millionth Grateful Dead fan to attend a Grateful Dead concert at the Meadowlands Sports Complex, including arena attendance.

June 5 - July 13, 1994

Men's World Cup :: A grass field was installed for 7 soccer matches held at the stadium during the Men's World Cup.

December 5, 1993

Army-Navy Game :: Army defeated Navy 16-14 in their second battle at Giants Stadium.

Summer of 1994

A Record-setting 15 Concerts in One Stadium :: Giants Stadium set the bar even higher with 15 shows in one summer: Billy Joel & Elton John (5 shows), Rolling Stones (4 shows), Pink Floyd, Grateful Dead and The Eagles (2 each), Attendance: 836,631.

October 5, 1995

Pope John Paul II Celebrated Mass at Giants Stadium :: Giants Stadium's all-time attendance record for a single event was set at 82,848 as a steady rain during the ceremony broke a New Jersey drought.

December 13, 1998

The New York Giants defeat the 13-0 Denver Broncos.

April 20, 1996

The first... MetroStars Game :: In their first game in franchise history, the MetroStars were defeated by the New England Revolution, 1-0.

June 19, 1999

Women's Soccer World Cup :: The tournament opened at Giants Stadium with Opening Ceremonies and two matches. Team USA defeated Denmark 3-0 and Brazil beat Mexico 7-1.

July 20, 1996

The Three Tenors in Concert :: Plácido Domingo, José Carreras, Luciano Pavarotti

January 10, 1999

New York Jets Divisional Playoff Game Victory :: The New York Jets defeated the Jacksonville Jaguars 34-24 and advanced to the AFC Championship Game.

1990

January 7, 2001

New York Giants Divisional Playoff Victory :: The New York Giants defeated the Philadelphia Eagles 20-10 in the NFC Divisional Playoffs Round.

July 15 - August 31, 2003

Bruce Springsteen & The E Street Band :: The band breaks its own record with 10 sold-out shows on The Rising Tour. Additionally, every show came complete with a Jersey Shore style boardwalk set up outside the stadium, fashioned with a carnival, sand castles, and a Ferris wheel.

July 7, 2007

Live Earth :: The concert was for the benefit of combating climate change and featured a live global broadcast through television, radio and internet. Presenters included Al Gore, Leonardo DiCaprio, Kevin Bacon, Cameron Diaz and Robert Kennedy, Jr. Performers included Dave Matthews Band, Bon Jovi, John Mayer, Fallout Boy, Keith Urban, The Police, Kelly Clarkson, Kanye West, The Smashing Pumpkins, Roger Waters and Alicia Keys.

January 4, 2003

The New York Jets Divisional Playoff Victory :: The Jets demolished the Indianapolis Colts 41-0 to move onto an AFC Divisional Playoff.

October 23, 2000

The Monday Night Miracle :: The New York Jets came back from a 30-7 deficit by scoring 30 points in the fourth quarter to beat the Miami Dolphins 40-37 in overtime.

September 19, 2005

The New Orleans Saints Home Game :: As the home team, the New Orleans Saints faced the New York Giants at Giants Stadium due to Hurricane Katrina, which caused the relocation of the game from the Louisiana Superdome.

September 24, 2009

The last U2 Concert :: U2's final Concert in the venue drew 84,472 fans, eclipsing the attendance mark Pope John Paul II set 14 years ago. At the end of the night, lead singer Bono issued his final tribute to a stadium as old as the band. He told the crowd, "It's a very special place for music, as well as the Giants."

2000

January 14, 2001

NFC Championship Game :: The New York Giants shut out the Minnesota Vikings 41-0 in the NFC Championship game to send the Giants to their third Super Bowl appearance.

February 11, 2001

The first... XFL Game in Giants Stadium :: The New York/New Jersey Hitmen lost their home opener, 19-12, to the Birmingham Thunderbolts.

Summer of 2003

A Record-Setting 16 Concerts in One Summer :: Bruce Springsteen and the E Street Band sold over 550,000 tickets during an incredible 10-show stand at Giants Stadium. Bon Jovi (2 shows), Z100's Zootopia, Hot 97 Summer Jam, Field Day Music Festival and the KROCK Summer Sanitarium Tour also rocked the venue that summer. Attendance: 851,364

July 31, 2003

Manchester United vs. Juventus :: A record 79,005 in attendance for a soccer game at Giants Stadium to see Manchester United defeat Juventus 4-1

August 18, 2007

David Beckham and the L.A. Galaxy :: 66,237 soccer fans attended an MLS match between the L.A. Galaxy and the New York Red Bulls, setting an attendance record for an MLS game that still stands today.

February 05, 2008

Super Bowl XLII Celebration :: The New York Giants returned home 2 days after toppling the 18-0 New England Patriots in Glendale, Arizona at Super Bowl XLII. The ceremony celebrated the third Giants Super Bowl victory in team history.

October 9, 2009

Bruce Springsteen & The E Street Band Concert :: For 3 hours and 9 minutes Bruce had taken to the stage for his 24th and final time in Giants Stadium. He played the entire "Born in the USA" album, the same one they played their first time at the stadium back in 1985. Closing with a final encore of "Jersey Girl" Giants Stadium officially had its last concert end at 11:36 pm.

9

GIANTS

What do you get when one of the most storied franchises in NFL

OPPOSITE: First game ever played at Giants Stadium on October 10, 1976. Unfortunately, the New York Giants lose to the Dallas Cowboys 24-14 in front of 76,042 fans. RON MOFFAT/STAR-LEDGER

history builds a place to call its own beginning on October 10, 1976? Three NFL Championships for starters. Not to mention numerous playoff berths behind greats like Taylor, Simms, Parcells, Hampton, Strahan, Barber, Toomer and Manning, to name just a few.

Let's not forget other memorable moments in Giants history at the stadium, such as the original "Gatorade shower," compliments of Jim Burt when he poured a cooler full of the sports drink on the head of Bill Parcells after their triumph over the Redskins in October 1985.

It has since turned into a tradition that has become a staple for winning teams across the NFL.

The home to the New York Giants has had its share of triumphs, and it's these recollections that will last a lifetime.

GIANTS
pro!
THE OFFICIAL MAGAZINE
OF THE N.F.L. & GAME PROGRAM
$1.00

RIGHT: The Giants enter the stadium as they play their first game ever at Giants Stadium. DEMETRIO JAREMENKO/STAR-LEDGER

FAR RIGHT: The Cowboys kick off to the Giants. MARK GREENBERG/STAR-LEDGER

OPPOSITE TOP: Larry Csonka breaks through a hole. MARK GREENBERG/STAR-LEDGER

OPPOSITE BOTTOM: Doug Kotar makes a cut behind some key blocks to pick up key yardage. Kotar would go on to lead the Giants in rushing during the 1976 season. DEMETRIO JAREMENKO/STAR-LEDGER

PREVIOUS TOP LEFT: Pat Summerall speaks at the opening of Giants Stadium. DEMETRIO JAREMENKO/STAR-LEDGER

PREVIOUS MIDDLE LEFT: Alex Webster and Mrs. Vincent Lombardi. DEMETRIO JAREMENKO/STAR-LEDGER

PREVIOUS BOTTOM LEFT: Bob Hope attends the opening game. DEMETRIO JAREMENKO/STAR-LEDGER

PREVIOUS MIDDLE: Opening ceremonies before the game. MARK GREENBERG/STAR-LEDGER

PREVIOUS TOP RIGHT: John Duncan of Clifton sells beer at the stadium. RON MOFFAT/STAR-LEDGER

PREVIOUS BOTTOM MIDDLE: Jack Cassidy of Jersey City sells programs. RON MOFFAT/STAR-LEDGER

PREVIOUS BOTTOM RIGHT: (L-R) Adrian Foley Jr., Former Gov. William Cahill, Sonny Werblin, Al Linkletter, and Aubrey Lewis. DEMETRIO JAREMENKO/STAR-LEDGER

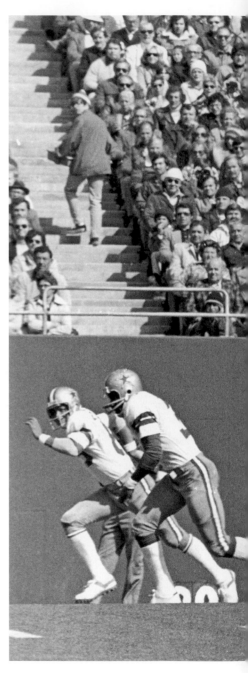

ABOVE: Leading up to the Giants' division game against the Redskins, coach Bill Parcells tried to motivate nose tackle Jim Burt by getting under his skin. On game day, after the Giants 17-3 win on October 20, 1985, Burt returns the favor: he dumps the Gatorade cooler on Parcells as the clock runs out. The Gatorade shower becomes an NFL tradition.
PIM VAN HEMMEN/STAR-LEDGER

LEFT: Giants vs. Redskins game action, October 20, 1985.
PIM VAN HEMMEN/STAR-LEDGER

FAR LEFT: Giants fans refer to the play as "The Fumble." Philadelphia Eagles fans call it "The Miracle at the Meadowlands". With the Giants up 17-12, quarterback Joe Pisarcik #9 fumbled a hand off to fullback Larry Csonka, allowing Eagles Herman Edwards to pick up the ball and run 26 yards for the winning score.
STEVE KLAVER/STAR-LEDGER

OPPOSITE: Giants vs. Eagles game action, November 19, 1978.
STEVE KLAVER/STAR-LEDGER

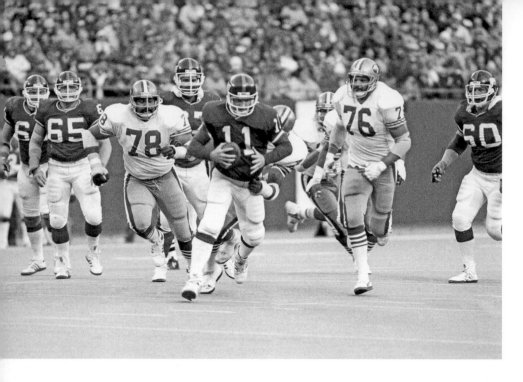

ABOVE: Phil Simms, December 29, 1985. The Giants play their first home playoff game at Giants Stadium, a 17-3 win over the Joe Montana-led 49ers. The Giants go on to lose to the Bears , 21-0, in the divisional round. PIM VAN HEMMEN/STAR-LEDGER

RIGHT: Jim Burt of the NY Giants celebrates after they win.
PIM VAN HEMMEN/STAR-LEDGER

FAR RIGHT: The Giants mascot cheers his team to a victory against the 49ers. PIM VAN HEMMEN/STAR-LEDGER

OPPOSITE: Giants' Lionel Manuel and Receivers Coach Pat Hodgson leave the field after their win, December 29, 1985. JENNIFER LAWSON/STAR-LEDGER

ABOVE: Phil Simms addresses the crowd at Giants Stadium January 27, 1987 during the Giants Super Bowl Victory Celebration. The Super Bowl XXI champion Giants and MVP Phil Simms are welcomed home by 45,000 snow-ball-throwing, kazoo-playing fans who braved 13-degree weather for the outdoor celebration. PIM VAN HEMMEN/STAR-LEDGER

LEFT: Bill Parcells holds up the Vince Lombardi Trophy to show it to fans who gathered during the Giants Super Bowl Victory Celebration.
PIM VAN HEMMEN/STAR-LEDGER

FAR LEFT: Fans take to the field as they attend the Super Bowl Vistory Celebration to welcome their team home.
RICHARD RASKA/STAR-LEDGER

21

RIGHT: Carl Banks #58, Everson Walls #28, and Lawrence Taylor #56 at the Meadowlands, during the NFC Division Playoff game between the Bears and Giants, January 13, 1991. JOE GIGLI/STAR-LEDGER

OPPOSITE TOP LEFT: Giants' Howard Cross #87 crossing the goal line after a touchdown. JOHN O'BOYLE/STAR-LEDGER

OPPOSITE BOTTOM LEFT: Giants' Ottis Anderson flying over Bears' Mark Carrier #20 and Richard Dent #95. JOHN O'BOYLE/STAR-LEDGER

OPPOSITE RIGHT: Giants' Ottis Anderson waving to the fans after the game. JOHN O'BOYLE/STAR-LEDGER

BELOW: The NY Giants play the Chicago Bears in a playoff game, January 13, 1991. JOE GIGLI/STAR-LEDGER

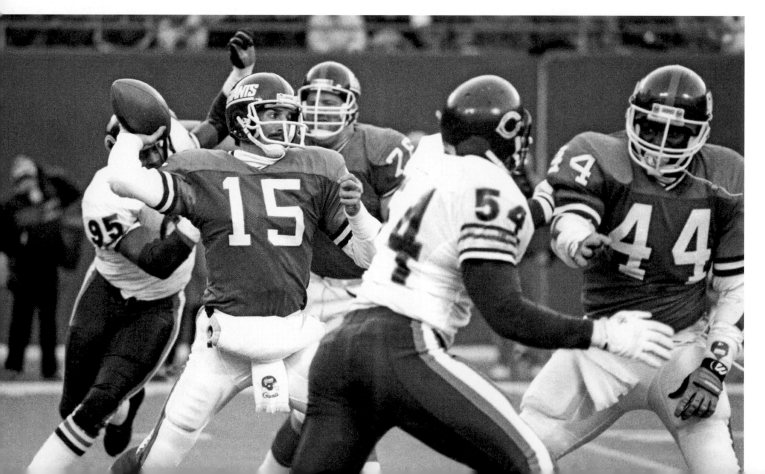

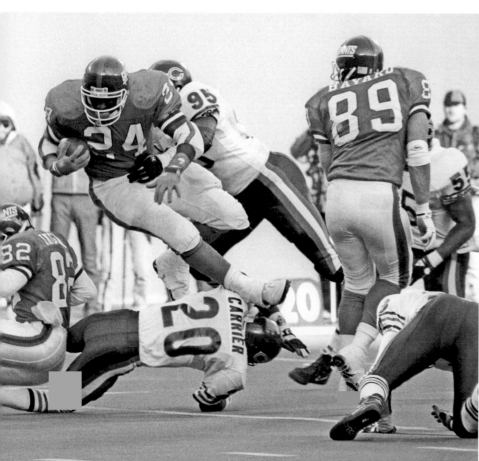

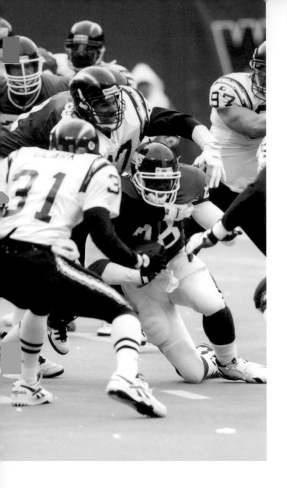

ABOVE: Giants #81 Amani Toomer holds up the winning touchdown in the fourth quarter to put the Giants over the Broncos 19-16. (Final score was 20-16). The Giants defeated the 13-0 Denver Broncos, December 13, 1998. MICHAEL SYPNIEWSKI/STAR-LEDGER

LEFT: Giants' #21 Tiki Barber celebrates the first touchdown in the first quarter (also #81 Amani Toomer and #30 Charles Way). MICHAEL SYPNIEWSKI/STAR-LEDGER

OPPOSITE TOP LEFT: The Giants running back Tyronne Wheatley #28 tries to get away from the Chargers #57 Dennis Gibson and #31 Willie Clark in second-quarter action. The Giants take on the San Diego Chargers, December 23, 1995. WILLIAM PERLMAN/STAR-LEDGER

OPPOSITE BOTTOM LEFT: Phil Simms, who spent his full 15-year NFL career with the Giants, has his No. 11 jersey officially retired in a ceremonial presentation by Giants Owner, Wellington Mara during halftime of the season-opener against Dallas on September 4, 1995. He also throws one more pass, a 30 yard hook up with former teammate Lawrence Taylor. The two-time Super Bowl champion exits in a convertible to triumphant applause. MATT RAINEY/STAR-LEDGER

OPPOSITE RIGHT: The Giants #94 Michael Brooks tackles Chargers #24 Aaron Hay-don as he tries to get around his teammate #86 Alfred Pupunu in second-quarter action, December 23, 1995. WILLIAM PERLMAN/STAR-LEDGER

ABOVE: Giants #31 Jason Sehorn makes an interception in front of the Eagles #80 Torrance Small in the first half. Sehorn got up and ran for a TD on the play. The New York Giants hosted the Philadelphia Eagles in the NFC divisional playoff on January 7, 2001. TIM FARRELL/STAR-LEDGER

LEFT: Giants Jesse Armstead #98 points toward the crowd after sacking Donovan McNabb.
ANDREW MILLS/STAR-LEDGER

FAR LEFT: Jesse Armstead #98 (left) and Keith Hamilton #75, (obscured) dump Gatorade on the head of coach Jim Fassel after the Giants win.
ANDREW MILLS/STAR-LEDGER

OPPOSITE: Giants Ron Dixon carries the ball as he sprints to a touchdown on the opening play of the first quarter, January 7, 2001. Closing in is Eagles Je'Rod Cherry #25. TIM FARRELL/STAR-LEDGER

ABOVE: The New Orleans Saints play as the home team against the Giants at Giants Stadium on Sept. 19, 2005. New Orleans Super Dome was damaged after Hurricane Katrina in late August 2005, leaving the Saints without a home stadium. CHRIS FAYTOK/STAR-LEDGER

RIGHT: Fans hold up a banner prior to the game. CHRIS FAYTOK/THE STAR-LEDGER

FAR TOP RIGHT: The Giants' Jeremy Shockey gets out in front of the Saints secondary to make the catch. CHRIS FAYTOK/STAR-LEDGER

FAR BOTTOM RIGHT: Giants #17 Plaxico Burress reaches for a poorly thrown ball in the first half during the game. CHRIS FAYTOK/STAR-LEDGER

OPPOSITE: Saints #26 Deuce McAllister shares a moment with former President George H.W. Bush prior to the game. CHRIS FAYTOK/STAR-LEDGER

JETS

On September 6, 1985, the New York Jets joined the Giants in a unique

partnership that placed two professional NFL teams within the same stadium. They felt right at home, often earning back-to-back seasons of playoff appearances. They've continued their playoff tradition culminating with a spectacular playoff run that brought them to the AFC Championship game in their final season at Giants Stadium.

Another stand-out memory came on a Monday night in October of 2000. Down by 23 points at the end of the third quarter, the Jets launched an aerial and ground assault against division opponent Miami Dolphins, to win in overtime 40-37. This is just one example of their unshaken resolve. But one of the most cherished stories of perseverance came when former Jet Dennis Byrd, who was temporarily paralyzed the previous season, walked out to midfield at the opening game of the 1993 season for the honorary coin-toss. Standing ovations by spectators and players alike cemented Byrd as a model of determination that reached far beyond Jets fans.

These memories and more have given fans from near and far reason to embrace their beloved Jets.

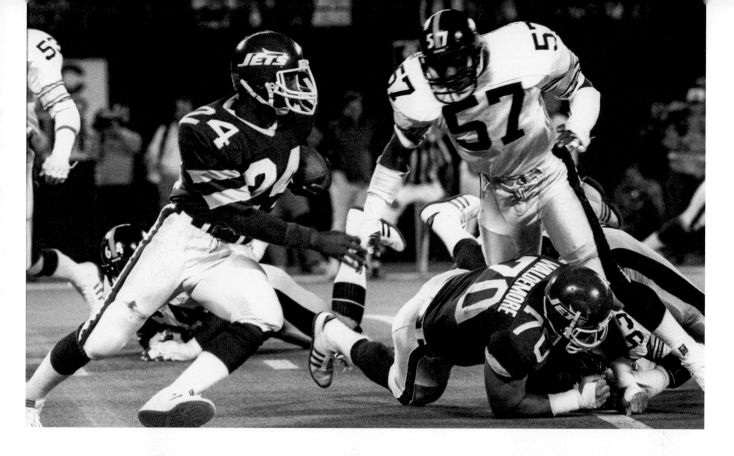

TOP: September 6, 1984: The Jets first home game at Giants Stadium. The Jets Freeman McNeil runs around the Pittsburgh Steelers defense. The Jets ultimately lose 23-17.
MARK ABRAHAM/STAR-LEDGER

BOTTOM LEFT: Jets QB Pat Ryan is sacked by Pittsburgh's Keith Willis during the same home opener.
MARK ABRAHAM/STAR-LEDGER

BOTTOM RIGHT: Jets Mark Gastineau sacks Steeler QB David Woodley during the second quarter of the game.
MARK ABRAHAM/STAR-LEDGER

OPPOSITE: Jets Bobby Humphrey stops for a cut during the return against the Steelers. MARK ABRAHAM/STAR-LEDGER

FOLLOWING LEFT: Tailgaters at the Jets first playoff game at Giants Stadium on December 28, 1985. From left to right: Jim Wargo of Rahway, Rich Cacchion of Edison, Jack Wargo of Rahway and John Lepore of Avenel. The Jets lost to the New England Patriots 26-14. BOB GURECKI/STAR-LEDGER

FOLLOWING TOP RIGHT: Mickey Shuler #82 of the Jets beats out Andre Tippett for a Jets TD in the third quarter of the game. RICH KRAUSS/STAR LEDGER

FOLLOWING BOTTOM RIGHT: Referee Jerry Seesn separates Patriots Cedric Jones and Jets Davlin Mullen. Jones was ejected for unsportsmanlike conduct.
RICH KRAUSS/STAR-LEDGER

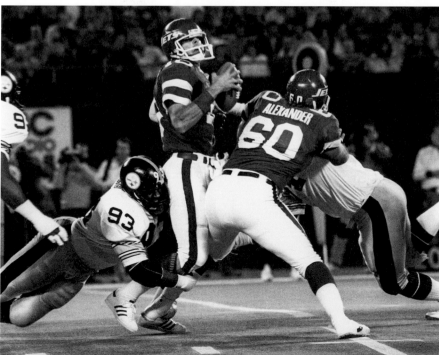

33

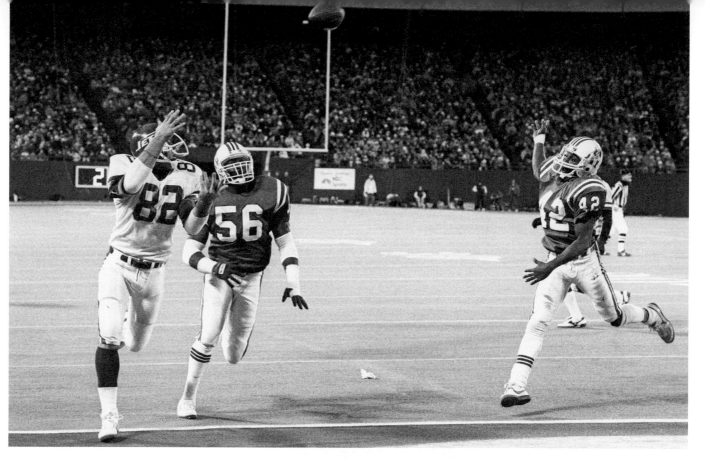

ABOVE: Ronnie Lott pulls down this interception as the Jets go on to win 17-12 vs the Cincinnati Bengals. The win left fans feeling good as they also were celebrating their 25th anniversary of the Super Bowl III Jets team at the game. GEORGE MCNISH/STAR-LEDGER

LEFT: Jets Hall of Fame quarterback Joe Namath waves to the crowd at Giants Stadium, November 21, 1993, during a special 25th anniversary celebration of the 1969 Super Bowl III team that beat the then Baltimore Colts. GEORGE MCNISH/STAR-LEDGER

OPPOSITE LEFT: Former Jets defensive end Dennis Byrd returns to Giants Stadium, September 5, 1993, where a head-first collision left him with a broken neck and partial paralysis nearly a year earlier. Told he would never walk again, Byrd strides to midfield with his former teammates for the season-opening coin toss. At half-time, the team presents him with the Dennis Byrd Trophy which will be given each year to the Jets' most inspirational player. "I must say that I miss the lights, adrenaline, and most of all the cheers," he says. "But God has given me many things to be thankful for." GEORGE MCNISH/STAR-LEDGER

OPPOSITE RIGHT: Byrd receives a hug from teammate Chris Burkett during his return to participate in the season-opening coin toss. GEORGE MCNISH/STAR-LEDGER

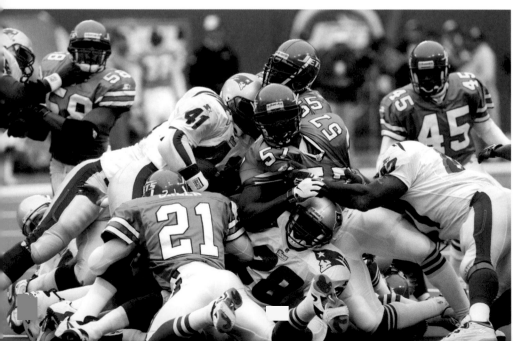

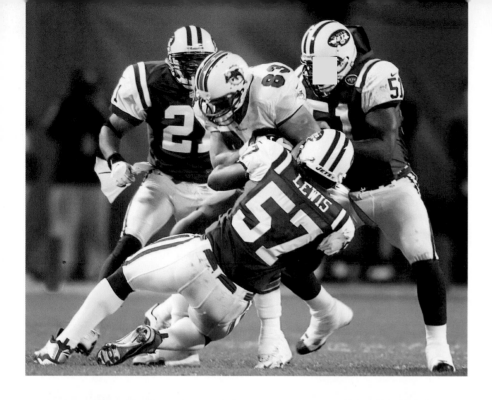

OPPOSITE TOP: Jets defensive back Raymond Austin #36 and Aaron Glenn celebrate Austin's play against the Patriots during second half.
GEORGE MCNISH/STAR-LEDGER

OPPOSITE BOTTOM LEFT: The Jets defense stacks up Keith Byars on a short yardage play on third down in the fourth quarter at Giants Stadium, October 19, 1997. GEORGE MCNISH/STAR-LEDGER

OPPOSITE BOTTOM MIDDLE: Patriots QB Drew Bledsoe is sacked by Victor Green during fourth quarter action play at Giants Stadium, October 19, 1997. GEORGE MCNISH/STAR-LEDGER

OPPOSITE BOTTOM RIGHT: A proud fan showing his support during the Jets vs. Patriots game.
GEORGE MCNISH/STAR-LEDGER

ABOVE: NY Jets receiver Jermaine Wiggins (celebrates after a TD pass from Vinny Testaverde) during the fourth quarter in a conference game vs. the Miami Dolphins on October 23, 2000. The game came to be known as the "Monday night miracle." JOE EPSTEIN/STAR-LEDGER

TOP LEFT: New York Jets defenders Mo Lewis #57 Bryan Cox #51 and Victor Green #21 team up to bring down Miami Dolphins receiver Hunter Goodwin #83 during the first quarter.
JOE EPSTEIN/STAR-LEDGER

LEFT: Dolphins Derrick Rodgers brings down Jets Richie Anderson during the third quarter as the Jets go on to beat the Maimi Dolphins in overtime, 40-37.
JOHN O'BOYLE/STAR-LEDGER

39

TOP: Jets #94 John Abraham puts pressure on Colts QB #18 Peyton Manning during the AFC wildcard playoff game between the New York Jets and the Indianapolis Colts at Giants Stadium, January 4, 2003. JOHN O'BOYLE/STAR-LEDGER

BOTTOM LEFT: Jets quarterback Vinny Testaverde looks on intensely from the sideline. WILLIAM PERLMAN/STAR-LEDGER

BOTTOM RIGHT: Jets coach Herman Edwards greets Colts coach Tony Dungy before the game. JOHN O'BOYLE/STAR-LEDGER

OPPOSITE LEFT: Jets #20 Richie Anderson scores the first TD of the game during the first quarter.
JOHN O'BOYLE/STAR-LEDGER

OPPOSITE TOP RIGHT: Jets Richie Anderson #20 gives the number 1 finger as he congratulates Lamont Jordan #34 after he scores a touchdown to make the score 40-0 in the fourth quarter.
WILLIAM PERLMAN/STAR-LEDGER

OPPOSITE BOTTOM RIGHT: The Jets Chad Pennington #10 celebrates after the Jets 41-0 win.
WILLIAM PERLMAN/STAR-LEDGER

TOP: Tom Cruise takes a photo with Jets fans before the start of the game.
NOAH K. MURRAY/STAR-LEDGER

ABOVE: The New York Jets hosted the Washington Redskins at Giants Stadium, August 16, 2008.
NOAH K. MURRAY/STAR-LEDGER

RIGHT: Kellen Clemens scrambles for a first down during the Jets vs. Washington game. NOAH K. MURRAY/STAR-LEDGER

OPPOSITE: Jets quarterback Brett Favre attempts a pass against Redskins defender Marcus Washington #53 in the first quarter of the Jets vs. Redskins game. NOAH K. MURRAY/STAR-LEDGER

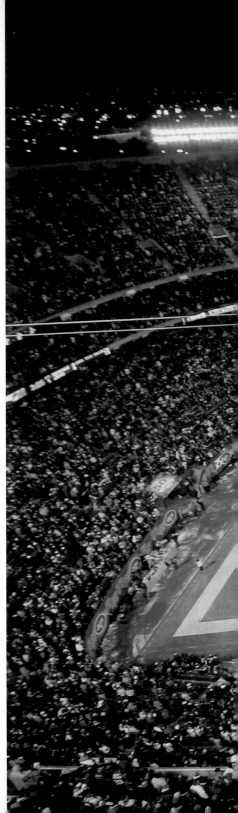

ABOVE: Fans walk in front of the New Meadowlands Stadium as they make their way into Giants Stadium, January 3, 2010. The Jets play the Cincinnati Bengals in the final NFL football game at Giants Stadium which will be demolished in the following months.
TONY KURDZUK/STAR-LEDGER

TOP RIGHT: A group of Jets fans from Staten Island outside Giants Stadium as the New York Jets prepare to host Cincinnati. ANDREW MILLS/STAR-LEDGER

BOTTOM RIGHT: Former Jet Vinny Testaverde is honored during half time. The New York Jets play the Cincinnati Bengals in the last regular season football game, January 3, 2010.
JENNIFER BROWN/STAR-LEDGER

FAR RIGHT: A giant American flag is unfurled for the National Anthem before the start of the game as seen from atop the press box, January 3, 2010.
TONY KURDZUK/STAR-LEDGER

44

ABOVE: Jets corner Darrelle Revis #24 has Chad Ochocinco #85 covered like a glove on a deep pass early in the first quarter. ANDREW MILLS/STAR-LEDGER

TOP LEFT: Jets Head Coach Rex Ryan and quarterback Mark Sanchez react after Kerry Rhodes picked up a fumble by Bengals quarterback J.T. O'Sullivan in the fourth quarter. TONY KURDZUK/STAR-LEDGER

LEFT: Jets quarterback Mark Sanchez is greeted by Fireman Ed Anzalone, who said, "I love you, kid. I love you." as Sanchez takes a victory lap around the entire perimeter of the stadium after the Jets beat the Bengals to earn a spot in the playoffs. ANDREW MILLS/STAR-LEDGER

OPPOSITE: Jets Brad Smith #16 breaks a pair of tackles and heads for the end zone for a touchdown on a QB keeper/option play in the second quarter. ANDREW MILLS/STAR-LEDGER

SPORTS

No one could argue that there's more to this place than NFL teams. Through the years, Giants Stadium has hosted terrific games and matches, such as World Cup soccer, college football and lacrosse. It has

also become the main stage for thousands of New Jersey high-school football players over the years who strive to win a championship each December for their schools.

But one particular moment in 1977 transcends sports lure. On October 1, soccer legend, Pele, played his final game in Giants Stadium. What made it even more unique was that he took the field for the

Cosmos in the first half, and then closed out his career by playing for Santos. While Pele bid farewell in 1977, the 1999 FIFA Women's World Cup was just the beginning for Team USA during the opening round held at the stadium. Team USA would go on to win Gold for our country and put women's soccer on center stage for fans everywhere. Giants Stadium also ushered in a new college football

tradition – trading in the "Garden State Bowl" at the end of the season. New Jersey introduced the "Kickoff Classic" and became the first to officially start the college football season.

Home to the Cosmos, MetroStars and then Red Bulls soccer teams, the world-caliber talent that played on the field over the years could fill a hall of fame.

ABOVE: Roberta Flack sings at the opening ceremony of Pele's last game at Giants Stadium on October 1, 1977. DEMETRIO JAREMENKO/STAR-LEDGER

TOP: Pele in action during his last game. He played the first half with the Cosmos and the second half with his former team, Santos. DEMETRIO JAREMENKO/STAR-LEDGER

LEFT: Pele bids farwell to over 60,000 fans. DEMETRIO JAREMENKO/STAR-LEDGER

OPPOSITE: One of many Pele fans in attendance for his final game. DEMETRIO JAREMENKO/STAR-LEDGER

TOP: Westfield Cheerleaders practice leading up to the kick-off between Westfield and Barringer in the State Sectional Finals, December 3, 1977.
BILL COCO/STAR-LEDGER

BOTTOM LEFT: Cosmos #9 Giorgio Chunaglia chases the ball during the season-opening game at Giants Stadium, April 17, 1977. VIC YEPELLO/STAR-LEDGER

BOTTOM RIGHT: The North American Soccer League's Cosmos play their first game in Giants Stadium, beating the Rochester Lancers 2-0.
VIC YEPELLO/STAR-LEDGER

OPPOSITE: No. 1 Westfield defeated No. 2 Barringer 33-12 in the Section 2, Group 4 title game. The game drew 33,000 fans - a record crowd for a high school football game in New Jersey.
BILL COCO/STAR-LEDGER

ABOVE: Rutgers' #30 Glen Kehler is chased by Arizona's #92 Tom Allen at the first Garden State Bowl on December 16, 1978. Rutgers loses to Arizona State 34-18, in what was also the first bowl appearance in the Scarlet Knights' history. Three more Garden State Bowls - which welcomed players with Broadway shows, Christmas shopping on Fifth Avenue and even a beauty pageant - were played at Giants Stadium before the game was replaced by the pre-season Kickoff Classic. RON MOFFAT/STAR-LEDGER

RIGHT: The Cosmos win the Soccer Bowl defeating the Tampa Bay Rowdies, 3-1, for their second straight Soccer Bowl championship at Giants Stadium August 27, 1978. STEVE KLAVER/STAR-LEDGER

FAR RIGHT: The Cosmos in action on their way to winning the Soccer Bowl against the Rowdies. STEVE KLAVER/STAR-LEDGER

LEFT: Temple University fullback Mark Bright (30) tries to escape the hold of California linebacker Stan Holloway during the Garden State Bowl, December 15, 1979. MARK ABRAHAM/STAR-LEDGER

OPPOSITE: Rutgers Albert Ray (L with ball) runs for a short gain with Alabama's Thomas Boyd (90) and Tommy Wilcox (15) in pursuit. Rutgers nearly stuns No. 1 ranked Alabama in what could have been one of the program's greatest upsets. The Scarlet Knights lose, 17-13, but afterward Crimson Tide coach Bear Bryant says, "We didn't beat Rutgers. All I can say is we won." MARK ABRAHAM/STAR-LEDGER

ABOVE: Notre Dame QB Blair Kiel #5 during a play. Navy takes on Notre Dame at Giants Stadium November 1, 1980. RICHARD CHU/STAR-LEDGER

TOP RIGHT: Navy cheerleaders on the sidelines. RICHARD CHU/STAR-LEDGER

RIGHT: Garden State Bowl III half-time ceremonies, December 14, 1980. Houston takes on Navy. RICHARD CHU/STAR-LEDGER

OPPOSITE: A sea of Navy Midshipmen attend the Navy vs. Notre Dame game. RICHARD CHU/STAR-LEDGER

ABOVE: The Soviet Union's Oleg Blokhin #3 of the Europe Team moves the ball around Argentina's Diego Maradona #10 of the World Team at the All-Star Soccer Game held at Giants Stadium, August 7, 1982. JERRY MCCREA/STAR-LEDGER

LEFT: Fans of individual teams unite for a day as the World Team takes on the Europe Team at the FIFA World All Star soccer game at Giants Stadium.
JERRY MCCREA/STAR-LEDGER

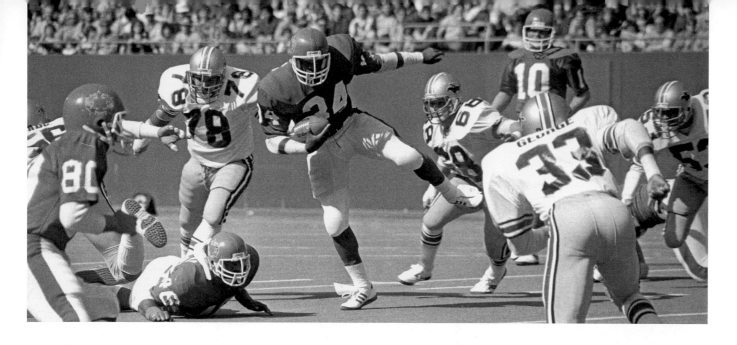

ABOVE: New Jersey Generals of the United States Football League play their first game at Giants Stadium against the Tampa Bay Bandits, March 20, 1983. STEVE BOOTH/STAR-LEDGER

TOP LEFT: Heisman Trophy winner Herschel Walker carries the ball for the Generals, March 20, 1983. They lose to the Tampa Bay Bandits, 32-9. STEVE BOOTH/STAR-LEDGER

BOTTOM LEFT: Penn State's Jon Williams #44 looks for running room against Nebraska during first-half action at the inaugural Kickoff Classic, August 29, 1983. Defending national champion Penn State loses to preseason No. 1 Nebraska 44-6. The Kickoff Classic, which is the first college football game ever held in August, is played for the next 20 years. STEVE BOOTH/STAR-LEDGER

OPPOSITE: Mike Rozier of Nebraska (#30 with ball) and #66 John Sherlock at the first Kickoff Classic, August 29, 1983. BILL CLARK/STAR-LEDGER

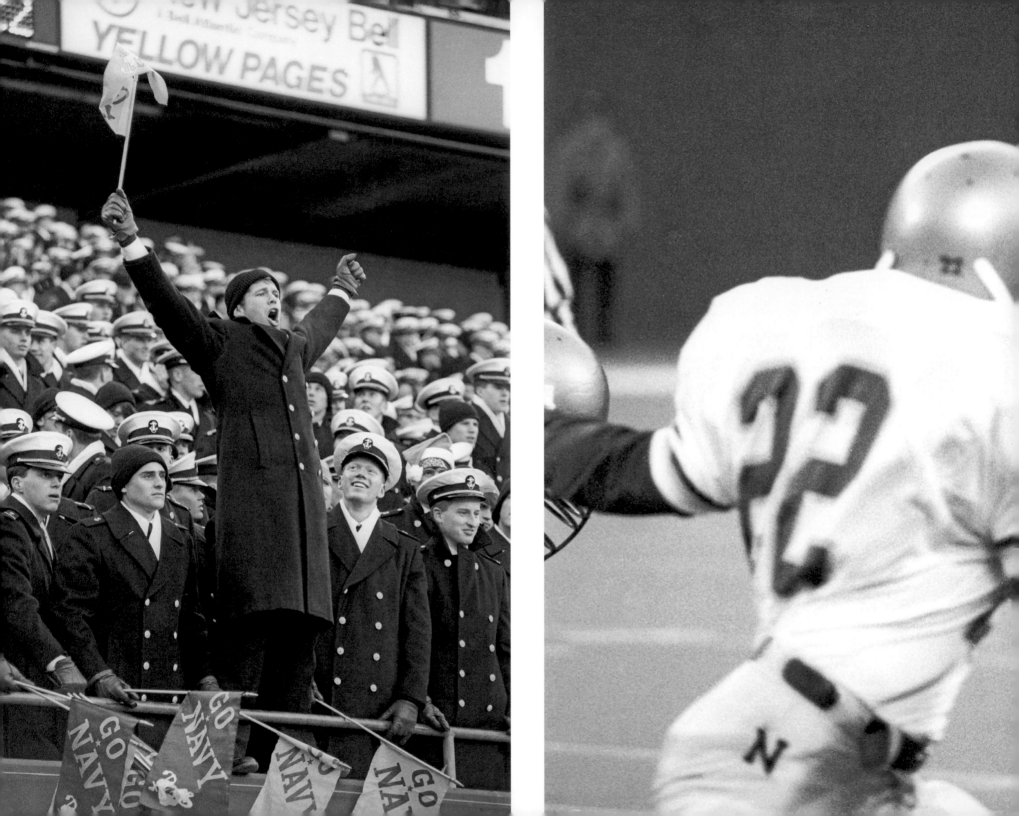

ABOVE: Navy's Bob Weissenfels #42 brings down Army's Callian Thomas #42. Navy came from behind to win 19-17 on a 32 yard field goal from kicker Frank Schenk with 11 seconds left. The Army - Navy game was first played at Giants Stadium on December 9, 1989 but the rivalry event returned three more times. JOHN O'BOYLE/STAR-LEDGER

LEFT: Army cadets show their support during the rivaled Army-Navy game. JOHN O'BOYLE/STAR-LEDGER

FAR LEFT: Army's Bryan McWilliams #9 tries to elude Chris Cordero #22. JOHN O'BOYLE/STAR-LEDGER

OPPOSITE: A Navy midshipman stands out from the crowd with his enthusiastic support for Navy. JOHN O'BOYLE/STAR-LEDGER

ABOVE: Terry Smith #8 of Penn State moves through the Georgia Tech secondary after catching a Tony Sacca pass for thirty yards during first quarter action in Kickoff Classic IX at Giants Stadium, August 28, 1991. The Nittany Lions defeated co-national champion Georgia Tech 34-22 before 77,409 - then the biggest crowd ever to watch college football at Giants Stadium. GEORGE MCNISH/STAR-LEDGER

RIGHT: Ken Swilling #8 and Tom Johnson #1 of Georgia Tech leap to block a point after a touchdown attempt by Penn State kicker Scott Sisson during the first quarter action. GEORGE MCNISH/STAR-LEDGER

OPPOSITE LEFT: Georgia Tech QB Shawn Jones #10 lets a pass fly during first quarter action against Penn State. GEORGE MCNISH/STAR-LEDGER

OPPOSITE RIGHT: Georgia Tech coach Bobby Ross talks with his quarterback Shawn Jones on the sideline during a timeout. GEORGE MCNISH/STAR-LEDGER

TOP: The MetroStars' Andrew Restrepo #20 takes the ball as the New England Revolution's Welton #11 tries to stop him in the first half action in East Rutherford.
ED CURRY/STAR-LEDGER

BOTTOM: The MetroStars' Miles Joseph #19 and the Revolution's Richard Weiszmann fight for the ball.
ED CURRY/STAR-LEDGER

FAR RIGHT: New England's Geoff Aunger #6 and Welton pursue Metro-Stars' Matt Knowles #3 as he charges towards the New England net in first half action. ED CURRY/STAR-LEDGER

OPPOSITE TOP: A MetroStars fan waves a flag in the stands.
ED CURRY/STAR-LEDGER

OPPOSITE BOTTOM: MetroStars' #5 Nicola Caricola battles New England's #19 Rob Ukrop during game play.
PATTI SAPONE/STAR-LEDGER

TOP: The 1994 FIFA World Cup, the world's most prestigious soccer tournament, came to the United States in the Summer of 1994. Seven games, including the Italy vs. Bulgaria semi-final, were held at Giants Stadium before sold-out crowds. The great success of the tournament in the United States led to the creation of Major League Soccer, a professional soccer league which started play in 1996. BILL KOSTROUN/NJSEA

BOTTOM LEFT: The opening ceremony before the first World Cup game to be played at Giants Stadium. A very lively crowd of 75,338 fans saw Ireland defeat Italy 1-0 on June 18, 1994. Ray Houghton's goal ensured that Ireland would gain revenge on Italy who had beaten them in the quarter-finals of the previous World Cup. BILL KOSTROUN/NJSEA

BOTTOM MIDDLE: Norway goalkeeper Erik Thorstvedt picks the ball out of the air saving a free kick during Group E pool play against Italy, June 23, 1994. BILL KOSTROUN/NJSEA

BOTTOM RIGHT: Italy salvaged an important 1-0 victory against Norway on a header in the 69th minute by Dino Baggio, despite playing most of the game without Roberto Baggio, their star, and at a one-man disadvantage. June 23, 1994 BILL KOSTROUN/NJSEA

OPPOSITE: The "Ole Ole Ole Ole" soccer anthem rang out non-stop from the stands at Giants Stadium during the Italy vs. Ireland match. BILL KOSTROUN/NJSEA

ABOVE: Portuguese soccer star Luis Figo dribbles the ball in the first half of play for his team Real Madrid. Spanish soccer team Real Madrid plays AC Roma in soccer action at Giants Stadium on August 8, 2002.
ARIS ECONOMOPOULOS/STAR-LEDGER

LEFT: USA's Mia Hamm scores her first goal against Denmark. The United States or Team USA takes on Denmark in the opening game of the 1999 FIFA Women's World Cup at Giants Stadium, June 19.
JOHN O'BOYLE/STAR-LEDGER

FAR LEFT: USA's Kristine Lilly celebrates her second half goal during the USA vs. Denmark game.
JOHN O'BOYLE/STAR-LEDGER

ABOVE: The Italian Super Cup is an annual pre-season soccer competition held the week before the season begins in Italy. It matches up the Serie A (Juventus) and Coppa Italia (A.C. Milan) winners from the previous season as a prelude to the new season. The match is usually played at the home of the Serie A champions but on August 3, 2003 the Italian Super Cup came to East Rutherford, NJ. Juventus defeated A.C. Milan on penalty kicks to capture the Italian Super Cup before a crowd of 54,128. BILL KOSTROUN/NJSEA

TOP RIGHT: Manchester United controls the ball en route to a 4-1 victory over Juventus. BILL KOSTROUN/NJSEA

BOTTOM RIGHT: Juventus and A.C. Milan fight for the ball. BILL KOSTROUN/NJSEA

OPPOSITE: A sellout crowd of 79,005 watched a matchup of European soccer powers at Giants Stadium. Manchester United beat Juventus 4-1 with Tim Howard, from North Brunswick, NJ, making his debut in goal for the English team after more than five seasons as the MetroStars' goalkeeper. BILL KOSTROUN/NJSEA

ABOVE: Fans play "pick-up" soccer games in the parking lot before the Red Bulls-Galaxy game. NOAH K. MURRAY/STAR-LEDGER

TOP LEFT: #9 Juan Pablo Angel heads the ball away from defender #2 Mike Randolph in the second half. NOAH K. MURRAY/STAR-LEDGER

TOP MIDDLE: David Beckham #23 and the Los Angeles Galaxy took on the New York Red Bulls in front of 66,237 in one of the most thrilling Major League Soccer games in history on August 18, 2007 to set an MLS regular-season attendance record. The Galaxy won 5-4. NOAH K. MURRAY/STAR-LEDGER

LEFT: Red Bulls fans are cheering it up for their team during the Red Bulls-Galaxy game. NOAH K. MURRAY/STAR-LEDGER

OPPOSITE: Landon Donovan of the L.A. Galaxy #10 and the Red Bulls' Joe Vide #14 go after the ball. NOAH K. MURRAY/STAR-LEDGER

ABOVE: Legendary Coach Eddie Robinson headed up the Grambling State football program for 57 years, where he won 408 games, most in NCAA history at the time he retired in 1997. Robinson coached the Tigers 10 times in the New York Urban League Classic at Giants Stadium.
BILL KOSTROUN/NJSEA

LEFT: The New York Urban League's annual football classic celebrates the life of Whitney M. Young, Jr. and benefits the New York Urban League's Scholarship Fund and its education programs. Morgan State defeated Winston-Salem State 16-10 in overtime in the 38th NYUL Football Classic, September 19, 2009. BILL KOSTROUN/NJSEA

OPPOSITE TOP: The NYUL Classic is not just a football game – there is just as much interest in the spectacular half-time show which features a battle of the bands. Winston-Salem State performs at half-time.
BILL KOSTROUN/NJSEA

OPPOSITE BOTTOM LEFT: The Winston-Salem State cheerleaders entertain the fans. BILL KOSTROUN/NJSEA

OPPOSITE BOTTOM RIGHT: The Morgan State Bears perform at half-time in the Battle of the Bands. BILL KOSTROUN/NJSEA

ABOVE: It was tough day for Lakeland fan Ashley Marion during the NJSIAA North I Jersey Group 3 football final against Wayne Hills High School Football on Saturday, December 6, 2008. ED MURRAY/STAR-LEDGER

TOP RIGHT: Lakeland's John Allard #1 is tackled by Wayne Hills' Matt DeBlock #80. ED MURRAY/STAR-LEDGER

BOTTOM RIGHT: Wayne Hills celebrates after their win with a pile-on in the endzone. ED MURRAY/STAR-LEDGER

FAR RIGHT: Steve Timko, Executive Director of the NJSIAA, presents Wayne Hills their victory trophy after their surprise win over Lakeland. ED MURRAY/STAR-LEDGER

TOP: On April 4, 2009, lacrosse had finally arrived at Giants Stadium. Six elite men's college lacrosse teams came to play in the inaugural Big City Classic. Among them they owned 24 national championships and 67 final four appearances. BILL KOSTROUN/NJSEA

ABOVE: North Carolina Attacker Bart Wagner #1 fights past Virginia defender Matt Kelly #33. BILL KOSTROUN/NJSEA

RIGHT: North Carolina rips a shot at Virginia goalie Adam Ghitelman. BILL KOSTROUN/NJSEA

LEFT: Syracuse attacker fights off a Princeton defender at the Big City Classic on April 4, 2009. BILL KOSTROUN/NJSEA

BOTTOM LEFT: Princeton attacker Jack McBride fights past the Syracuse defense. BILL KOSTROUN/NJSEA

BELOW: Virginia fans cheer the No. 1-ranked Cavaliers to a come-from behind victory over No. 10-ranked North Carolina. BILL KOSTROUN/NJSEA

RIGHT: Mexico's Gerardo Torrado #6 shoots the ball into the top right corner of the net against Team USA goalkeeper Troy Perkins to score on a penalty kick.
ARISTIDE ECONOMOPOULOS/STAR-LEDGER

BELOW: Fans arrive for the final international soccer match at Giants Stadium.
ARISTIDE ECONOMOPOULOS/STAR-LEDGER

TOP: Mexico defeated the United States 5-0 to win the CONCACAF Gold Cup in front of a sellout crowd of 79,156 at Giants Stadium, July 26, 2009.
ARISTIDE ECONOMOPOULOS/STAR-LEDGER

BOTTOM LEFT: Mexico's Jose Magallon #2 tries to stay on his feet and get to the ball. The United States fell short of winning a second consecutive Gold Cup title. ARISTIDE ECONOMOPOULOS/STAR-LEDGER

BOTTOM RIGHT: Mexico's Jose Castro #15 and Teams USA's Robert Rogers #7 battle for the ball.
ARISTIDE ECONOMOPOULOS/STAR-LEDGER

CONCERTS & SPECIAL EVENTS

What comes to mind when you think of Giants Stadium? Football, of course. But over the past three-plus decades, it's been about much more. What started as a diamond in the

swampy Meadowlands rough has been home to scores of mega-concerts and charity events, such as NetAid, Live Earth and a visit from Pope John Paul II. And we all know, there's nothing like a big league concert to bring people together. Giants Stadium has had more than its share of headliners – from every genre and generation – to grace the playing-field-turned-stage.

From the sold-out Springsteen homecoming shows, the Beach Boys and the Jackson Five Victory Tour to The Three Tenors, Rolling Stones, Billy Joel and everything in between. These greats all had one thing in common, the ability to rock the 756-foot long, 592-foot wide, and 144-foot high structure.

But performances aren't complete

without tailgating. And at Giants Stadium, it wasn't just the food that was memorable. One of the most notable parking lot performances was the re-creation of Michael Jackson's "Thriller."

Day in and day out, Giants Stadium was successfully transformed into a virtual concert arena – all 65,000 square feet. Cherish the memories....

OPPOSITE: Michael Jackson performs with his brothers at the Jackson Victory Tour at Giants Stadium in New Jersey July 29, 1984. RICK BOWME/STAR-LEDGER

ABOVE: Fans wait for The Beach Boys to perform the first concert at Giants Stadium on June 25, 1978. The line-up also included The Steve Miller Band, Pablo Cruise and Stanky Brown and brought over 62,000 to the new venue. VERNEST/STAR-LEDGER

RIGHT: Steve Miller belts out a song during his set as part of the Beach Boys concert. VERNEST/STAR-LEDGER

OPPOSITE: A shot of the crowd from the stage during one of The Steve Miller Band songs. VERNEST/STAR-LEDGER

ABOVE: Mike Love of the Beach Boys heads to the stage to start their set at Giants Stadium. VERNEST/STAR-LEDGER

LEFT: Jeannie Penkava of Bloomfield watched the concert. VERNEST/STAR-LEDGER

OPPOSITE: Mike Love gets the crowd on their feet with a classic Beach Boys song. VERNEST/STAR-LEDGER

FOLLOWING LEFT: The Grateful Dead perform their first concert at Giants Stadium September 2, 1978. Lead vocals and guitar, the main figure of the band, Jerry Garcia (on right) walks with the band's drummer Micky Hart towards the stage just before they played. STEVE KLAVER/STAR-LEDGER

FOLLOWING RIGHT: The Grateful Dead about to perform at their first concert in Giants Stadium. STEVE KLAVER/STAR-LEDGER

NO SMOKING

RUNNING ORDER

11:00-11:50 New Riders

11:50-12:20 Set Change

12:20-1:35 Willie Nelson

1:35-

2:05

ABOVE: Ann Wilson (L) and her sister Nancy Wilson (R) of the rock group Heart. Music in the Meadowlands drew over 60,000 on September 15, 1980. The Eagles, Heart and the Little River Band perform at the day-long "Music in the Meadowlands," following the release of The Eagles' "The Long Run" album. MARK ABRAHAM/STAR-LEDGER

TOP: Tom Chafatelli of Roselle Park sits on the shoulders of his friend Chris Gilliland of East Brunswick during the show. MARK ABRAHAM/STAR-LEDGER

RIGHT: The Eagles on stage at the Music in the Meadowlands concert. MARK ABRAHAM/STAR-LEDGER

OPPOSITE: Madonna brought her "Who's That Girl" world tour to Giants Stadium on August 9, 1987, playing to a sold-out crowd of over 56,000 fans. BILL KOSTROUN/NJSEA

ABOVE: Michael Jackson performs with his brothers at the Jackson Victory Tour at Giants Stadium, July 29, 1984. RICK BOWME/STAR-LEDGER

LEFT: Michael Jackson mixes his trademark dance moves on stage with unmistakable vocals during the concert. RICK BOWME/STAR-LEDGER

OPPOSITE: A view from the crowd at the Jackson Victory Tour concert. BOB GURECKI/STAR-LEDGER

PREVIOUS LEFT: The "Young Creative People" of Newark perform for the people waiting in line at the Jackson Victory Tour. BOB GURECKI/STAR-LEDGER

PREVIOUS MIDDLE: Diane Moretto of Lyndhurst buys her four tickets. BOB GURECKI/STAR-LEDGER

PREVIOUS TOP RIGHT: Scott Smith (left) and his brother Devonn of Neptune pose with their Michael Jackson gloves. BOB GURECKI/STAR-LEDGER

PREVIOUS MIDDLE RIGHT: Anthony Dewitt of Newark, a member of the "Young Creative People," entertains the crowd as they wait to get into the stadium. BOB GURECKI/STAR-LEDGER

PREVIOUS BOTTOM RIGHT: Mr. and Mrs. Mel Hantman (Leah) of Maplewood show off their Jackson tour tickets. BOB GURECKI/STAR-LEDGER

RIGHT: Sue Schubauer of Stirling and Kristen Weisul of Stirling tailgating in the parking lot, September 1, 1985. Bruce Springsteen and The E Street Band played six dates in Giants Stadium during their Born in the U.S.A. Tour. Riding the popularity of the "Born in the U.S.A." album, they make the bold jump to professional football stadiums - fronted by a buffer, tougher Springsteen - and impressively sell them out.
KATHLEEN D. WHELAN/STAR-LEDGER

FAR RIGHT: Tailgating in the parking lot, September 1, 1985 before Bruce Springsteen and The E Street Band play six sold-out shows in Giants Stadium during their Born in the U.S.A. Tour.
KATHLEEN D. WHELAN/STAR-LEDGER

RIGHT: The group Peter, Paul & Mary performs at A Conspiracy of Hope concert, June 15, 1986. A Conspiracy of Hope Tour concludes with a sold-out, 11-hour concert headlined by U2, Sting and a reunion of The Police. The tour makes six stops across the country, marking the 25th anniversary of Amnesty International and the human rights it has supported.
BOB GURECKI/STAR-LEDGER

BOTTOM RIGHT: Marc Fuoti of New Brunswick enjoys himself with the music in the upper deck at A Conspiracy of Hope concert, June 15, 1986.
BOB GURECKI/STAR-LEDGER

OPPOSITE LEFT: The group Third World performs at the concert.
BOB GURECKI/STAR-LEDGER

OPPOSITE RIGHT: A concert-goer holds up a sign of what the concert is all about. BOB GURECKI/STAR-LEDGER

BELOW: Elaine Ross of High Park (foreground) cools off under the shower provided at the Meadowlands during the concert. BOB GURECKI/STAR-LEDGER

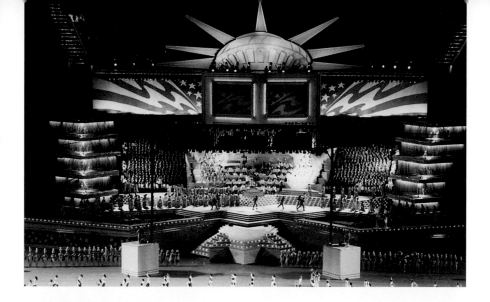

ABOVE & RIGHT: A four day celebration of the Statue of Liberty's centennial and restoration, called Liberty Weekend, culminates with closing ceremonies at the Meadowlands. Muhammad Ali, Billie Jean King, Hank Aaron, an Olympic skating exhibition, the French equestrian team and 200 Elvis impersonators are part of the festivities, held at both Meadowlands Arena and Giants Stadium, July 6, 1986. ROBERT EBERLE/STAR-LEDGER

OPPOSITE: An overhead shot of Giants Stadium as it sits on the Meadowlands Sports Complex. Meadowlands Arena and Meadowlands Racetrack can be seen in the background. BILL KOSTROUN/NJSEA

ABOVE: Bono sings to the masses during the U2 concert at Giants Stadium on September 14, 1987. GENE BOYARS/STAR-LEDGER

RIGHT: The Edge scans the crowd during the Giants Stadium show, part of the Joshua Tree tour. GENE BOYARS/STAR-LEDGER

FAR RIGHT: The crowds are excited to see U2. GENE BOYARS/STAR-LEDGER

OPPOSITE: Paul McCartney rocked Giants Stadium during two sold-out shows on July 9 & 11, 1990. The "Paul McCartney World Tour" marked his first major concert outing in ten years and was McCartney's first tour under his name. BILL KOSTROUN/NJSEA

ABOVE: Genesis brought their "We Can't Dance" tour to Giants Stadium, playing to over 97,000 fans during shows on June 2 & 3, 1992. BILL KOSTROUN/NJSEA

RIGHT: The Grateful Dead, fronted by the late Jerry Garcia, played two sold-out dates on August 3 & 4 during the record-setting 15 concerts of 1994. BILL KOSTROUN/NJSEA

OPPOSITE: Billy Joel & Elton John played to 293,539 fans during five sold-out shows at Giants Stadium in July 1990 as part of their "Face 2 Face" tour. BILL KOSTROUN/NJSEA

ABOVE: Roger Daltrey takes the microphone at The Who concert on June 29, 1989. The Who played four shows in five days at Giants Stadium drawing a total of 223,135 fans.
JOHN O'BOYLE/STAR-LEDGER

LEFT: Pete Townshend behind the guitar. JOHN O'BOYLE/STAR-LEDGER

OPPOSITE: (L-R) Brian Schuele, 17, Mike Romano, 17, and Steven Dillon, 17, of Edison cook up burgers and hot dogs while tailgating in the parking lot before The Who concert.
STEVE GOLECKI/STAR-LEDGER

FOLLOWING SPREAD: Pope John Paul II celebrated Mass in the pouring rain at Giants Stadium setting an attendance record of 82,948. The faithful created a colorful scene wearing rain ponchos to protect themselves from the torrential downpour.
FRANK H. CONLON/STAR-LEDGER

ABOVE: The Three Tenors, Placido Domingo, Jose Carreras and Luciano Pavorotti perform along with Conductor James Levine, Saturday July 20, 1996. ED CURRY/STAR-LEDGER

TOP RIGHT: The Rolling Stones brought their "Bigger Bang" tour to Giants Stadium on September 15, 2005. Mick Jagger works the crowd in classic style. BILL KOSTROUN/NJSEA

BOTTOM RIGHT: The stage for the "Bigger Bang" tour stood 84-feet tall with multiple levels of built-in seating. 400 lucky fans watched the show from these on-stage seats. BILL KOSTROUN/NJSEA

OPPOSITE The Rolling Stones "A Bigger Bang" tour rocked Giants Stadium on September 15, 2005, bringing their 84-foot tall multi-level stage to life with on-stage seating for 400 lucky fans. BILL KOSTROUN/NJSEA

TOP RIGHT: In July and August 2003, Bruce Springsteen and the E Street Band rocked Giants Stadium for an unprecedented 10 show stand. BILL KOSTROUN/NJSEA

FAR TOP RIGHT: Crowds pack the Meadowlands Boardwalk in the Summer of 2003. BILL KOSTROUN/NJSEA

FAR BOTTOM RIGHT: Fans play beach volleyball at the Meadowlands Boardwalk. BILL KOSTROUN/NJSEA

BOTTOM: Another great night of rock and roll. Pictured (l to r): Nils Lofgren, Clarence Clemons, Max Weinberg, Bruce Springsteen, Steve Van Zandt, Patti Scialfa, Garry Tallent. BILL KOSTROUN/NJSEA

OPPOSITE: To celebrate the 10 show stand, an authentic Jersey Shore boardwalk was constructed at the Meadowlands. Fans had the chance to enjoy a ride on a Ferris wheel, listen to Jersey bands, eat their fill of hot dogs, cotton candy, salt water taffy and soft-serve ice cream, hang out with friends and then go into Giants Stadium for a great night of music. BILL KOSTROUN/NJSEA

RIGHT: Jersey-bred rockers Bon Jovi visited Giants Stadium for three sold out dates in July 2006. BILL KOSTROUN/NJSEA

BOTTOM RIGHT: Bon Jovi thanks the Giants Stadium crowd for a successful three-day stand during which they entertained 164,975 fans. BILL KOSTROUN/NJSEA

BELOW: Jon Bon Jovi plays to his hometown crowd. BILL KOSTROUN/NJSEA

ABOVE: The Police participated in an all-star lineup at the historic Live Earth event on July 7, 2007. Part of a series of benefit concerts, Giants Stadium was one of eleven locations around the world to host events on this day. BILL KOSTROUN/NJSEA

TOP LEFT: The Dave Matthews Band performed in this historic concert event which was broadcast to a mass global audience through television, radio and live internet streams. BILL KOSTROUN/NJSEA

FAR LEFT: Alicia Keys performs at Giants Stadium during Live Earth 2007. Live Earth was founded by Al Gore and Kevin Wall with a primary mission of combating climate change. BILL KOSTROUN/NJSEA

BOTTOM LEFT: A flying pig takes up the cause as it floats over Giants Stadium during the Live Earth concert on July 7, 2007. BILL KOSTROUN/NJSEA

ABOVE: U2 played their final stand at Giants Stadium on September 23 & 24, 2009. Drummer Larry Mullen Jr. performs as Bono sings behind him.
ARISTIDE ECONOMOPOULOS/STAR-LEDGER

RIGHT: U2 guitarist the Edge plays during the September 23 show.
ARISTIDE ECONOMOPOULOS/STAR-LEDGER

FAR RIGHT: U2 singer Bono, left, performs with bassist Adam Clayton.
ARISTIDE ECONOMOPOULOS/STAR-LEDGER

OPPOSITE: U2 bassist Adam Clayton shares the spotlight with guitarist the Edge during a song.
ARISTIDE ECONOMOPOULOS/STAR-LEDGER

ABOVE & LEFT: Bono continues to bring intensity to U2's concerts - as he does here at their last stand at Giants Stadium. The September 23 show was attended by 84,472 fans, breaking the all-time stadium attendance record previously set by Pope John Paul II in 1995 (82,948). ARISTIDE ECONOMOPOULOS/STAR-LEDGER

ABOVE & TOP LEFT: AC/DC's "Black Ice World Tour" played Giants Stadium on July 31 during the final concert season at the venue. KEN BACHOR

BOTTOM LEFT: Mary J Blige performs during the 2009 Hot 97 concert as part of a line-up that also included T Pain, Young Jeezy and Jadakiss among others and was hosted by "Saturday Night Live" alum Tracy Morgan. BILL KOSTROUN/NJSEA

ABOVE: Detail photograph of the big screen over the stage, after Bruce Springsteen and the E Street Band performed the last concert at Giants Stadium Friday night, October 9, 2009. They ended the show with, "American Land," and "Jersey Girl." SAED HINDASH/STAR-LEDGER

TOP: 6-year-old Georgia Finley of West Hartford, CT hangs out with her mom Christine in the rear of their car before seeing her first concert, Bruce Springsteen and The E Street Band, September 30, 2009. TONY KURDZUK/STAR-LEDGER

LEFT: Eddie Gomez (front) and Flavio Jawor of West New York have fun throwing a football in the parking lot, before the concert. TONY KURDZUK/STAR-LEDGER

RIGHT: The large monitors display the words to "Wrecking Ball," a song Springsteen wrote especially for the venue. TONY KURDZUK/STAR-LEDGER

OPPOSITE LEFT: Max Weinberg keeps the beat. TONY KURDZUK/STAR-LEDGER

OPPOSITE RIGHT: Saxophonist Clarence Clemons, guitarist Nils Lofgren and keyboardist Charles Giordano jam on stage during the show. TONY KURDZUK/STAR-LEDGER

FOLLOWING LEFT: Bruce Springsteen belts out one familiar tune after another during the last concert. TONY KURDZUK/STAR-LEDGER

FOLLOWING RIGHT: Fireworks light up Giants Stadium as Bruce Springsteen and The E Street Band perform, October 2, 2009. SAED HINDASH/STAR-LEDGER

BELOW: Bruce Springsteen and The E Street Band perform the last concert at Giants Stadium, October 9, 2009. They ended the show with, " American Land," and "Jersey Girl." BILL KOSTROUN/NJSEA